Homestyle
Family Favorites

45 quick-and-easy recipes your family will love

Here are 10 of our favorite easy dinner menus. Each menu gives you an entrée and a side dish or dessert recipe; then we fill in with easy ideas for you to round out the meal. Along with each menu, look for a grocery list and prep plan that will provide an easy pace for getting dinner on the table.

weeknight menus

A Taste of Tex-Mex

Weeknight Enchiladas   refried beans

shredded lettuce with guacamole   **Toffee Surprise**

serves 4

Weeknight Enchiladas

prep: 7 minutes   cook: 29 minutes

1   pound ground chuck
1   small onion, chopped
1   (10¾-ounce) can tomato soup, undiluted
1   (10-ounce) can mild enchilada sauce
8   (7- or 8-inch) flour tortillas
2   cups (8 ounces) shredded Cheddar cheese, divided
Sour cream (optional)
Sliced ripe olives (optional)

Cook beef and onion in a large skillet over medium-high heat until meat is browned, stirring until it crumbles; drain and return to skillet.
Stir soup and enchilada sauce into meat mixture. Spread ¼ cup meat mixture onto each tortilla; sprinkle tortillas evenly with 1 cup cheese. Roll up tortillas; place, seam side down, in a greased 13- x 9-inch baking dish. Pour remaining meat mixture over tortillas.
Cover and bake at 350° for 20 minutes. Uncover and sprinkle with remaining 1 cup cheese; bake 5 more minutes or until cheese melts. If desired, serve with sour cream and olives. Yield: 4 servings.

Toffee Surprise

prep: 9 minutes

1   quart vanilla ice cream
4   (1¼-ounce) English toffee candy bars, coarsely crushed
¼   cup coffee liqueur

Spoon ice cream and crushed toffee bars evenly into 4 parfait glasses or dessert dishes. Just before serving, top each with 1 tablespoon liqueur. Yield: 4 servings.

menu plan

1. Prepare Toffee Surprise, but don't add liqueur; freeze until serving time.
2. Prepare and bake enchiladas.
3. While enchiladas bake, shred lettuce, and heat refried beans with green chiles in a saucepan over low heat.
4. Sprinkle cheese on enchiladas; bake 5 more minutes.
5. Top each dessert with liqueur just before serving.

groceries needed

- 1 pound ground chuck
- 1 small onion
- 1 (10¾-ounce) can tomato soup
- 1 (10-ounce) can mild enchilada sauce
- Package flour tortillas
- 8 ounces Cheddar cheese
- Sour cream
- Can sliced ripe olives
- 1 quart vanilla ice cream
- 4 (1¼-ounce) English toffee candy bars
- ¼ cup coffee liqueur
- 1 (16-ounce) can refried beans
- 1 (4.5-ounce) can chopped green chiles
- Lettuce
- Commercial guacamole

equipment needed

- Large skillet
- 13- x 9-inch baking dish
- Saucepan

Sunset Supper

Herbed Shrimp and Pasta   sliced tomatoes
Dilled Garlic Bread   pound cake

serves 6

Herbed Shrimp and Pasta

prep: 5 minutes   cook: 20 minutes

     8 ounces dried angel hair pasta, uncooked
     1 cup butter
1 ½ pounds peeled, medium-size fresh shrimp (2 pounds
        unpeeled)
     4 garlic cloves, minced
     2 cups half-and-half
   ½ cup chopped fresh parsley
   ½ teaspoon salt
   ¼ teaspoon pepper
     2 teaspoons chopped fresh dill or ¾ teaspoon dried
        dillweed (optional)
     Garnish: fresh dill sprigs

Cook pasta according to package directions. Drain; set aside, and keep warm.

Meanwhile, melt butter in a large heavy skillet over medium-high heat; add shrimp and garlic. Cook, stirring constantly, 3 to 5 minutes or until shrimp turn pink. Remove shrimp, and set aside, reserving garlic and butter in skillet.

Add half-and-half to skillet; bring to a boil, stirring gently. Reduce heat, and simmer 15 minutes or until thickened, stirring occasionally. Add shrimp, parsley, salt, pepper, and, if desired, chopped dill; stir until blended. Serve over pasta. Garnish, if desired. Yield: 6 servings.

Dilled Garlic Bread

prep: 10 minutes   cook: 10 minutes

   ⅓ cup butter or margarine, softened
   ¼ cup finely chopped fresh dill
     2 large garlic cloves, crushed
     1 (16-ounce) loaf unsliced French bread
   ¼ cup grated Parmesan cheese

Combine first 3 ingredients. Slice loaf in half lengthwise. Spread butter mixture evenly on cut sides of bread. Sprinkle with cheese. Place on an ungreased baking sheet. Bake at 375° for 10 minutes or until browned. Slice and serve hot. Yield: 1 loaf.

menu plan

1. Bring pasta water to a boil.
2. Soften butter for bread.
3. Cook pasta; keep warm.
4. While pasta cooks, prepare shrimp cream sauce.
5. Prepare and bake garlic bread.
6. Slice tomatoes and pound cake just before serving.

groceries needed

Check staples: butter or margarine, salt, pepper
- 8 ounces dried angel hair pasta
- 1 ½ pounds peeled, medium-size fresh shrimp
- Fresh garlic
- 2 cups half-and-half
- Bunch fresh parsley
- Bunch fresh dill
- 1 (16-ounce) loaf unsliced French bread
- ¼ cup grated Parmesan cheese
- Fresh tomatoes
- Pound cake

equipment needed

- Dutch oven
- Colander
- Large heavy skillet
- Baking sheet

Casual Night

Three-Pepper Pork Cutlets   rice pilaf with vegetables
fried apples   broccoli spears   **Cinnamon Ice Cream**

serves 4

Three-Pepper Pork Cutlets

prep: 10 minutes   cook: 8 minutes

1   (1-pound) pork tenderloin
1   teaspoon paprika
1   teaspoon dried thyme
½   teaspoon dried oregano
½   teaspoon dried rosemary, crushed
¼   teaspoon salt
¼   teaspoon ground white pepper
¼   teaspoon black pepper
⅛   teaspoon ground red pepper
1   teaspoon olive oil
2   garlic cloves, crushed

Cut pork crosswise into 12 slices. Place each pork slice between 2 sheets of heavy-duty plastic wrap, and flatten to ¼-inch thickness, using the heel of your hand or a meat mallet.

Combine paprika and next 9 ingredients; rub over both sides of pork slices. Place pork on a broiler rack coated with cooking spray; place rack in a broiler pan. Broil 5½ inches from heat 3 to 4 minutes on each side or until done. Yield: 4 servings.

Cinnamon Ice Cream

prep: 10 minutes

1   quart vanilla ice cream, slightly softened
1   teaspoon ground cinnamon
Hot fudge topping

Stir together ice cream and cinnamon in a large bowl. Refreeze, if desired. Scoop into serving dishes, and drizzle with fudge topping. Yield: 4 servings.

menu plan

1. Soften ice cream, and stir in cinnamon; freeze until serving time.
2. Cook rice pilaf and broccoli according to package directions; keep warm.
3. While side dishes cook, prepare pork, and broil.
4. Heat apples in a saucepan over medium-low heat, if desired.
5. Scoop ice cream into serving dishes, and top with fudge sauce before serving dessert.

groceries needed

Check staples: paprika, dried thyme, dried oregano, dried rosemary, salt, ground white pepper, black pepper, ground red pepper, olive oil, vegetable cooking spray, ground cinnamon
- 1 pound pork tenderloin
- Fresh garlic
- 1 (16-ounce) bag frozen rice pilaf with vegetables
- 1 (28-ounce) jar fried apples
- 1 (16-ounce) package frozen broccoli spears
- 1 quart vanilla ice cream
- Hot fudge topping

equipment needed
- Meat mallet
- Broiler pan with rack
- Saucepan with lid

Family-Pleasing Chicken

Creamy Chicken Casserole

green beans   **Mandarin Orange and Lettuce Salad**   apple pie

serves 4

Creamy Chicken Casserole

prep: 5 minutes   cook: 30 minutes

3   cups chopped cooked chicken
1   (10¾-ounce) can cream of chicken soup, undiluted
1   (8-ounce) carton sour cream
1   tablespoon poppy seeds
1½ cups crushed round buttery crackers (40 crackers)
¼   cup butter or margarine, melted

Combine first 4 ingredients; spoon into a greased 11- x 7-inch baking dish. Combine crushed crackers and butter, and sprinkle over chicken mixture. Bake, uncovered, at 350° for 30 minutes. Yield: 4 servings.

Mandarin Orange and Lettuce Salad

prep: 5 minutes

6   cups torn mixed greens or 1 (16-ounce) package
     mixed lettuces
1   (11-ounce) can mandarin oranges, drained
⅓   cup golden raisins
1   (2-ounce) package cashew nuts, toasted (⅓ cup)
½   cup commercial Italian dressing or sweet-and-sour
     dressing

Combine first 4 ingredients in a salad bowl. Pour salad dressing over salad, and toss. Serve immediately. Yield: 4 servings.

menu plan

1. Prepare and bake chicken casserole.
2. While casserole bakes, trim and cook green beans, and toast cashews for salad.
3. Prepare salad.
4. Heat pie during dinner.

groceries needed

Check staples: poppy seeds, butter or margarine
- 3 cups chopped cooked chicken
- 1 (10¾-ounce) can cream of chicken soup
- 1 (8-ounce) carton sour cream
- Round buttery crackers
- 6 cups torn mixed greens or 1 (16-ounce) package mixed lettuces
- 1 (11-ounce) can mandarin oranges
- ⅓ cup golden raisins
- 1 (2-ounce) package cashew nuts (⅓ cup)
- Commercial Italian or sweet-and-sour dressing
- 1½ pounds fresh or frozen green beans
- Commercial apple pie

equipment needed
- 11- x 7-inch baking dish
- Saucepan

Italian Fare

Quick Carbonara
green salad   rolls   **Simple Tiramisù**

serves 4

Quick Carbonara

prep: 10 minutes   cook: 19 minutes

1 (8-ounce) package dried spaghetti, uncooked
8 slices bacon
⅔ cup chopped green onions
1 (4-ounce) can sliced mushrooms, drained
3 egg yolks, lightly beaten
1½ cups (6 ounces) finely shredded Cheddar cheese
  Dash of pepper

Cook pasta according to package directions. Meanwhile, cook bacon in a large skillet until crisp; remove bacon, reserving 3 tablespoons drippings in skillet. Coarsely crumble bacon, and set aside.
Cook green onions and mushrooms in drippings in skillet over medium heat 2 minutes. Drain pasta, and place in a serving bowl. Stir egg yolks into hot pasta immediately after draining it. Stir in bacon, green onions and mushrooms, cheese, and pepper; toss. Serve immediately. Yield: 4 servings.

Simple Tiramisù

prep: 15 minutes   freeze: 30 minutes

1 (8-ounce) package cream cheese, softened
¾ cup strong brewed coffee, cooled
3 (1-ounce) squares semisweet chocolate, grated
¾ cup chopped almonds, toasted and divided
1 (12-ounce) container frozen whipped topping, thawed
2 (3-ounce) packages ladyfingers, split

Beat cream cheese in a large bowl at high speed of an electric mixer until fluffy. Add ¼ cup coffee, beating until blended. Stir in grated chocolate and ½ cup almonds. Set aside 1 cup whipped topping. Fold remaining whipped topping into cream cheese mixture.
Brush cut sides of ladyfingers with remaining ½ cup coffee. Arrange two-thirds of ladyfingers on bottom and up sides of a 2-quart bowl (such as a large mixing bowl); spoon cream cheese mixture into center. Top with remaining ladyfingers and reserved 1 cup whipped topping; sprinkle with remaining ¼ cup almonds. Cover and freeze 30 minutes. Yield: 8 servings.

menu plan

1. Bring pasta water to a boil.
2. Prepare tiramisù; freeze until serving time.
3. Cook pasta. Cook bacon.
4. While pasta cooks, toss salad ingredients, and finish preparing carbonara.
5. Heat rolls in oven according to package directions, if desired.

groceries needed

Check staples: 3 egg yolks, pepper
- 1 (8-ounce) package dried spaghetti
- 8 slices bacon
- Bunch green onions
- 1 (4-ounce) can sliced mushrooms
- 6 ounces Cheddar cheese
- 1 (8-ounce) package cream cheese
- Coffee
- 3 to 4 (1-ounce) squares semisweet chocolate
- ¾ cup chopped almonds
- 1 (12-ounce) container frozen whipped topping
- 2 (3-ounce) packages ladyfingers
- Makings for green salad
- Crusty rolls

equipment needed
- Dutch oven
- Colander
- Large skillet
- Electric mixer
- Pastry brush

Patio Supper

Sausage-Stuffed French Loaf   Cucumber-Tomato Salad

potato chips   chocolate chip cookies

serves 4

Sausage-Stuffed French Loaf

prep: 11 minutes   cook: 29 minutes

1   (16-ounce) loaf unsliced French bread
½   pound ground pork sausage
½   pound ground chuck
1   medium onion, chopped
2   cups (8 ounces) shredded mozzarella cheese
1   large egg, lightly beaten
¼   cup chopped fresh parsley
2   tablespoons Dijon mustard
½   teaspoon fennel seeds
½   teaspoon salt
¼   teaspoon pepper
2   tablespoons butter or margarine
1   large garlic clove, crushed

Cut off ends of loaf; set ends aside. Hollow out loaf with a long serrated bread knife, leaving a ½-inch shell. Process bread removed from inside loaf in a food processor to make coarse crumbs.

Cook sausage, beef, and onion in a large skillet until meat is browned, stirring until it crumbles; drain. Stir in 1 cup breadcrumbs, cheese, and next 6 ingredients. Spoon into shell; replace loaf ends, securing with wooden picks.

Melt butter in a saucepan. Add garlic; cook 1 minute. Brush garlic butter over loaf. Wrap loaf in foil, leaving top open slightly; place on a baking sheet. Bake at 400° for 25 minutes. Cut into 4 pieces. Yield: 4 servings.

Cucumber-Tomato Salad

prep: 8 minutes

3   tablespoons olive oil
1½   tablespoons lemon juice
1   teaspoon Dijon mustard
⅛   teaspoon salt
⅓   cup sliced ripe olives
2   tomatoes, cut into wedges
1   cucumber, sliced
      Lettuce leaves

Combine first 4 ingredients, stirring well with a fork or small whisk. Combine olives, tomato, and cucumber in a bowl. Pour dressing mixture over tomato mixture; toss. Cover and chill 30 minutes, if desired. Serve on lettuce leaves. Yield: 4 servings.

menu plan

1. Bake cookies according to package directions up to 1 day ahead.
2. Prepare and bake stuffed sausage loaf.
3. While loaf bakes, prepare salad; cover and chill.

groceries needed

Check staples: egg, Dijon mustard, fennel seeds, salt, pepper, butter or margarine, olive oil

- 1 (16-ounce) loaf unsliced French bread
- ½ pound ground pork sausage
- ½ pound ground chuck
- 1 medium onion
- 8 ounces mozzarella cheese
- Bunch fresh parsley
- Fresh garlic
- 1½ tablespoons lemon juice
- ⅓ cup sliced ripe olives
- 2 tomatoes
- 1 medium cucumber
- Lettuce leaves
- Potato chips
- Refrigerated chocolate chip cookie dough

equipment needed

- Serrated bread knife
- Food processor (optional)
- Large skillet
- Small saucepan
- Pastry brush
- Baking sheet

Splurge Supper

Filet Mignon with Horseradish Gravy

mashed potatoes   steamed asparagus   **Greek Salad**

French bread   commercial cheesecake

serves 4

Filet Mignon with Horseradish Gravy

prep: 2 minutes   cook: 20 minutes

 4 (5-ounce) beef tenderloin steaks
¼ teaspoon salt
¼ teaspoon pepper
 1 (¾-ounce) package brown gravy mix
½ cup water
½ cup red wine
2½ tablespoons prepared horseradish
 1 (8-ounce) package sliced fresh mushrooms

Heat a heavy nonstick skillet over medium-high heat until hot. Sprinkle steaks with salt and pepper. Add steaks to hot skillet; cook 1 minute on each side. Place steaks in a greased small baking dish.

Add gravy mix and next 3 ingredients to skillet. Bring to a boil; reduce heat, and simmer, stirring constantly, until thickened. Stir in mushrooms. Pour mixture over steaks. Bake, uncovered, at 350° for 15 minutes or to desired doneness. Yield: 4 servings.

Greek Salad

prep: 14 minutes

 1 medium head iceberg lettuce, torn
 1 small purple onion, thinly sliced
½ cup pepperoncini salad peppers
½ cup kalamata olives
 4 ounces crumbled feta cheese
½ cup commercial red wine vinaigrette

Combine all ingredients in a salad bowl; toss gently. Serve immediately. Yield: 4 servings.

menu plan

1. Thaw cheesecake according to package directions.
2. Prepare filet mignon recipe.
3. Microwave potatoes; then mash them. (Or prepare instant mashed potatoes according to package directions.)
4. While steaks cook, trim and steam asparagus in a small amount of boiling water 6 to 8 minutes.
5. Toss salad at the last minute.

groceries needed

Check staples: salt, pepper, prepared horseradish
- 4 (5-ounce) beef tenderloin steaks
- 1 (¾-ounce) package brown gravy mix
- Red wine
- 1 (8-ounce) package sliced fresh mushrooms
- 1 head iceberg lettuce
- 1 small purple onion
- ½ cup pepperoncini salad peppers
- ½ cup kalamata olives
- 4 ounces feta cheese
- Red wine vinaigrette
- 4 baking potatoes or 1 box of instant mashed potatoes
- 1 pound fresh asparagus
- French bread
- Frozen cheesecake

equipment needed
- Heavy nonstick skillet
- Small baking dish
- Asparagus steamer

Before the Game

Speedy Chili Dogs   Easy Coleslaw

potato chips   brownies

serves 8

Speedy Chili Dogs

prep: 5 minutes   cook: 35 minutes

1   pound ground chuck
1   large onion, chopped (2 cups)
1   garlic clove, crushed
1   (15-ounce) can tomato sauce
2   tablespoons chili powder
¼   teaspoon salt
⅛   teaspoon pepper
1   cup water
8   frankfurters, cooked
8   hot dog buns, split and toasted
2   cups (8 ounces) shredded mild Cheddar cheese
Chopped green onions

Combine first 3 ingredients in a large skillet, and cook over medium-high heat until beef is browned, stirring until it crumbles; drain. Add tomato sauce and next 4 ingredients. Bring to a boil; cover, reduce heat, and simmer 25 minutes, stirring occasionally.

Place frankfurters in buns. Spoon chili mixture over frankfurters; top with cheese and green onions. Yield: 8 servings.

Easy Coleslaw

prep: 2 minutes

1   (16-ounce) package shredded coleslaw mix
1   (8-ounce) bottle coleslaw dressing*
¼   teaspoon salt
¼   teaspoon pepper

Combine all ingredients in a large bowl, tossing well. Serve immediately, or cover and chill. Yield: 6 cups.

*For coleslaw dressing, we used Kraft.

menu plan
1. Prepare coleslaw. Chill, if desired.
2. Cook beef mixture for chili dogs.
3. While beef mixture simmers, cook frankfurters.
4. Split and toast buns; assemble chili dogs.

groceries needed
Check staples: chili powder, salt, pepper
- 1 pound ground chuck
- 1 large onion
- Fresh garlic
- 1 (15-ounce) can tomato sauce
- 8 frankfurters
- 8 hot dog buns
- 8 ounces mild Cheddar cheese
- Bunch green onions
- Potato chips
- 1 (16-ounce) package shredded coleslaw mix
- 1 (8-ounce) bottle coleslaw dressing
- Brownies from a deli bakery

equipment needed
- Large skillet with lid
- Large saucepan

Faux-Fried Favorites

Oven-Fried Fish

zesty French fries   turnip greens   corn on the cob

Lemon Frappé

serves 4

Oven-Fried Fish

prep: 5 minutes   cook: 10 minutes

¼ cup white cornmeal
¼ cup fine, dry breadcrumbs
½ teaspoon salt
½ teaspoon paprika
1½ teaspoons chopped fresh dill or ½ teaspoon dried dillweed
⅛ teaspoon pepper
1 pound fresh or frozen fish fillets, thawed
⅓ cup milk
3 tablespoons butter or margarine, melted
Lemon wedges
Tartar sauce

Combine first 6 ingredients in a shallow dish. Dip fish fillets in milk, and dredge in cornmeal mixture. Place coated fish in a lightly greased 13- x 9-inch pan; drizzle with butter.
Bake at 450° for 10 minutes or until fish flakes easily when tested with a fork. Serve with lemon wedges and tartar sauce. Yield: 4 servings.

Lemon Frappé

prep: 4 minutes

1 (6-ounce) can frozen lemonade concentrate, undiluted
½ cup cold water
1 pint lemon sherbet or vanilla ice cream*
1 (12-ounce) can ginger ale

Combine first 3 ingredients in container of an electric blender; process until smooth, stopping once to scrape down sides. Pour into a serving pitcher; add ginger ale. Serve immediately. Yield: 4 cups.

*Plenty of lemon flavor prevails if you use vanilla ice cream in this slushy dessert beverage. **To make a Lime Frappé,** use a 6-ounce can limeade in place of lemonade concentrate.

menu plan

1. Bake French fries according to package directions. Bring water to a boil for corn, if cooking fresh ears.
2. Microwave turnip greens according to package directions; boil fresh corn, or cook frozen corn according to package directions.
3. While fries bake, prepare fish. Add fish to bake in oven during last 10 minutes fries bake.
4. Blend frappé after dinner.

groceries needed

Check staples: cornmeal, salt, paprika, pepper, milk, butter or margarine
- Fine, dry breadcrumbs
- Fresh or dried dillweed
- 1 pound fresh or frozen fish fillets
- 1 or 2 lemons
- Tartar sauce
- 1 (32-ounce) bag frozen French fries (we used Ore-Ida Zesties)
- 1 (10- or 16-ounce) package frozen turnip greens
- 4 ears of corn or 1 (16-ounce) package frozen corn
- 1 (6-ounce) can frozen lemonade concentrate
- 1 pint lemon sherbet or vanilla ice cream
- 1 (12-ounce) can ginger ale

equipment needed

- Shallow dish
- 13- x 9-inch pan
- Electric blender
- Baking sheet

Soup-and-Sandwich Night

Cream of Pimiento Soup
Grilled Ham and Cheese

serves 4

Cream of Pimiento Soup

prep: 2 minutes   cook: 20 minutes

1   (4-ounce) jar diced pimiento, undrained
3   tablespoons butter or margarine
3   tablespoons all-purpose flour
1   (14-ounce) can chicken broth
1½ cups half-and-half
2   teaspoons grated onion
½   teaspoon salt
¼   teaspoon hot sauce
Garnish: sour cream

Place pimiento in a blender; process until smooth, stopping once to scrape down sides. Set aside.
Melt butter in a heavy saucepan over low heat; add flour, stirring until smooth. Cook, stirring constantly, 1 minute. Gradually add broth and half-and-half to saucepan; cook over medium heat, stirring constantly, until thickened and bubbly.
Stir in pimiento, onion, salt, and hot sauce; cook over medium-low heat, stirring constantly, until heated. Garnish, if desired. Yield: 3½ cups.

Grilled Ham and Cheese

prep: 8 minutes   cook: 4 minutes

1   cup (4 ounces) shredded Monterey Jack cheese
1   cup (4 ounces) shredded Cheddar cheese
¼   cup mayonnaise
1   tablespoon prepared mustard
1   green onion, finely chopped
8   slices sandwich bread
4   slices sandwich ham
¼   cup butter or margarine, softened

Combine first 5 ingredients. Spread cheese mixture over 4 bread slices. Top each with a ham slice; top with remaining bread slices. Spread half of butter on tops of sandwiches. Invert sandwiches onto a hot nonstick skillet or griddle; cook over medium heat until browned. Spread remaining butter on ungrilled sides of sandwiches; turn and cook until browned. Yield: 4 servings.

menu plan
1. Prepare soup; keep warm.
2. Assemble sandwiches; grill sandwiches just before serving.

groceries needed
Check staples: butter or margarine, all-purpose flour, salt, hot sauce, mayonnaise, prepared mustard
- 1 (4-ounce) jar diced pimiento
- 1 (14-ounce) can chicken broth
- 1½ cups half-and-half
- Small onion
- Sour cream
- 4 ounces Monterey Jack cheese
- 4 ounces Cheddar cheese
- 1 green onion
- 8 slices bread
- Sandwich ham

equipment needed
- Electric blender
- Heavy saucepan
- Nonstick skillet or griddle

our favorite entrées

Here are 25 of our most popular main dishes ideal for busy weeknights. Enjoy a variety of entrées ranging from beef to shrimp to vegetarian. Look for food facts following each recipe.

Steak in Pepper Cream

prep: 3 minutes   cook: 19 minutes

 ¼ teaspoon salt
 2 (12-ounce) New York strip steaks (¾ inch thick)
 1½ tablespoons green peppercorns in liquid, drained
 2 tablespoons steak sauce
 2 tablespoons water
 1 cup whipping cream
 ¼ teaspoon ground pepper

Place a 10-inch cast-iron skillet over medium heat until hot; sprinkle salt in skillet. Place steaks over salt; cook 4 minutes on each side or until browned. Remove from skillet.

Combine peppercorns, steak sauce, and water in hot skillet; cook over medium heat, stirring constantly, to loosen browned bits from bottom of skillet. Stir in whipping cream and pepper.

Bring to a boil; reduce heat, and simmer, stirring constantly, 3 to 4 minutes or until slightly thickened. Add steaks; simmer 5 minutes or to desired doneness, stirring occasionally. Yield: 2 to 4 servings.

Green peppercorns can be found in small jars on the grocery shelf along with the pickles.

Shortcut Lasagna

prep: 15 minutes   cook: 46 minutes

1   pound ground beef
2   large garlic cloves, crushed
1   (28-ounce) jar spaghetti sauce
½   cup water
1   large egg, lightly beaten
1   (12-ounce) container cottage cheese
1½ teaspoons pepper
8   lasagna noodles, uncooked
1   (10-ounce) package frozen chopped spinach, thawed
    and drained
2   cups (8 ounces) shredded mozzarella cheese
½   cup grated Parmesan cheese

Crumble beef into a 2-quart glass bowl; add garlic. Microwave at HIGH 6 minutes or until browned, stirring beef once; drain. Stir in spaghetti sauce and water. Combine egg, cottage cheese, and pepper.

Spread ½ cup meat sauce in a 13- x 9-inch baking dish. Top with half each of uncooked noodles, cottage cheese mixture, spinach, meat sauce, and mozzarella cheese. Repeat layers, and cover with heavy-duty plastic wrap.

Microwave at HIGH 8 minutes; then microwave at MEDIUM (50% power) 30 to 32 minutes or until noodles are tender, turning dish occasionally.

Sprinkle with Parmesan cheese; cover and let stand 15 minutes before serving. Yield: 6 servings.

The shortcut? Not cooking the noodles before layering them. They soften as they bake in the lasagna.

Barbara's Big Juicy Burgers

prep: 20 minutes   cook: 18 minutes

 1 (11.5-ounce) can lightly tangy vegetable juice*
 3 white sandwich bread slices, torn into pieces
 3 pounds ground chuck or ground round
 1 large egg
1½ teaspoons salt
 1 teaspoon pepper
10 hamburger buns

Microwave vegetable juice in a glass bowl at HIGH 1 minute. Add bread pieces, and let cool. Combine, using hands.

Combine vegetable juice mixture, ground chuck, and next 3 ingredients. Shape into 10 patties.

Grill patties, covered with grill lid, over medium-high heat (350° to 400°) 6 to 8 minutes on each side or until beef is no longer pink.

Spray cut sides of buns with cooking spray; place buns, cut sides down, on grill rack; grill 2 minutes or until lightly browned. Serve hamburgers on buns. Yield: 10 servings.

*For testing purposes only, we used V8 for vegetable juice.

Shape the mixture into 12 patties for smaller **quarter-pound** burgers.

Sweet Sloppy Joes

prep: 5 minutes   cook: 23 minutes

1½ pounds ground beef
 1 small onion, chopped
 1 small green pepper, seeded and chopped
 1 (10¾-ounce) can tomato soup, undiluted
 1 (8-ounce) can tomato sauce
 1 cup ketchup
 2 tablespoons brown sugar
 1 tablespoon Worcestershire sauce
 1 teaspoon prepared mustard
 ⅛ teaspoon garlic powder
 4 sesame seed hamburger buns, toasted

Cook first 3 ingredients in a large skillet until beef is browned, stirring until it crumbles; drain. Stir in soup and next 6 ingredients; simmer 10 to 15 minutes, stirring often. Serve on toasted buns. Yield: 4 servings.

For a menu partner, pop commercial frozen onion rings into the oven while the sloppy joe mixture simmers.

Texas Stew

prep: 5 minutes   slow cook: about 5½ to 10½ hours

2   pounds beef tips, cut into 1-inch pieces
1   (14½-ounce) can Mexican-style stewed tomatoes, undrained
1   (10½-ounce) can condensed beef broth, undiluted
1   (8-ounce) jar medium or mild picante sauce
1   (10-ounce) package frozen whole kernel corn
3   carrots, cut into ½-inch slices
1   medium onion, cut into thin wedges
2   cloves garlic, minced
1   teaspoon ground cumin
½   teaspoon salt
⅓   cup water
¼   cup all-purpose flour

Combine first 10 ingredients in a 3- or 4-quart electric slow cooker. Cover and cook on HIGH 5 hours or on LOW 10 hours or until meat is tender.

Combine water and flour, stirring until smooth; stir into meat mixture in slow cooker. Cook stew, uncovered, on HIGH 15 minutes or until thickened, stirring often. Yield: 10 cups.

Let your slow cooker **cook dinner while you work.** Just heat some bread to serve alongside when you get home.

Chicken-Fried Steak

¾ cup all-purpose flour
¾ teaspoon salt
¼ teaspoon pepper
½ cup buttermilk
¾ teaspoon hot sauce
1 pound beef cube steaks
¼ cup plus 2 tablespoons vegetable oil, divided
2 tablespoons all-purpose flour
1 cup milk
¼ teaspoon salt
¼ teaspoon pepper

Stir together first 3 ingredients in a shallow dish. Combine buttermilk and hot sauce in a bowl. Dredge steaks in flour mixture; dip into buttermilk mixture, and dip again in flour mixture.

Heat ¼ cup oil in a large skillet over medium-high heat. Add steaks, and cook 5 minutes on each side. Remove from skillet. Drain steaks on paper towels.

Heat remaining 2 tablespoons oil in skillet; whisk in 2 tablespoons flour, and cook, whisking constantly, 5 minutes or until light golden brown. Gradually whisk in milk; cook, whisking constantly, over medium heat until thickened and bubbly (about 10 minutes). Stir in ¼ teaspoon salt and ¼ teaspoon pepper. Serve over steaks. Yield: 4 servings.

Double-dipping the steaks in the flour mixture makes this homestyle classic extracrispy.

Weeknight Pork Chops

prep: 5 minutes   cook: 24 minutes

6 (½-inch-thick) boneless pork loin chops
¼ teaspoon salt
¼ teaspoon pepper
1 tablespoon vegetable oil
1 cup orange juice
¼ cup dry sherry
1 (1-ounce) envelope dry onion soup mix
1 cup chopped fresh mushrooms
¼ cup whipping cream

Sprinkle pork chops evenly with salt and pepper.
Cook in hot oil in a heavy skillet over medium-high heat 2 minutes on each side or until browned.
Add orange juice and next 3 ingredients; bring to a boil. Cover, reduce heat, and simmer 15 minutes. Transfer chops to a serving platter; keep warm. Reserve drippings in skillet.
Stir whipping cream into reserved drippings; cook over medium-high heat, stirring constantly, 5 minutes or until thickened. Serve over chops. Yield: 3 servings.
prep: 5 minutes   marinate: 8 hours   grill: 20 minutes

A **creamy** mushroom sauce helps keep the meat **tender** and **tasty.**

Molasses-Grilled Pork Tenderloin

½ cup molasses
¼ cup coarse-grained Dijon mustard
2 tablespoons apple cider vinegar or white vinegar
1 teaspoon salt
4 (¾-pound) pork tenderloins

Combine first 4 ingredients; brush half of mixture over pork. Cover and chill 8 hours. Chill remaining molasses glaze.

Coat grill rack with cooking spray; place on grill over medium-high heat (350° to 400°). Place pork on rack; grill, covered with grill lid, 18 to 20 minutes or until a meat thermometer inserted into thickest portion registers 160°, turning once and basting with reserved molasses glaze during last 8 minutes. Yield: 8 servings.

Looking for a shortcut? Grill the tenderloins as soon as you've glazed them. **You don't have to marinate them.**

Sweet Jalapeño Ribs

prep: 30 minutes   slow cook: 5½ to 10½ hours

2   (16-ounce) cans pinto beans, drained
3   pounds country-style pork ribs, trimmed
½   teaspoon garlic powder
½   teaspoon salt
½   teaspoon pepper
1   medium onion, chopped
1   (10.5-ounce) jar red jalapeño pepper jelly
1   (5-ounce) bottle steak sauce*
2   jalapeño peppers, seeded and finely chopped
    (optional)

Place beans in a 4-quart electric slow cooker. Set aside.

Cut ribs apart; sprinkle with garlic powder, salt, and ½ teaspoon pepper. Place ribs on a rack in a broiler pan. Broil 5½ inches from heat 18 to 20 minutes or until well browned, turning once. Add ribs to slow cooker, and sprinkle with onion.

Combine jelly, steak sauce, and, if desired, chopped pepper in a saucepan; cook over low heat until jelly melts. Pour over ribs; stir gently.

Cover and cook on HIGH 5 to 6 hours or on LOW 9 to 10 hours. Remove ribs; skim fat from sauce. Cook sauce with beans, uncovered, on HIGH 30 more minutes or until slightly thickened. Add ribs just before serving to reheat. Yield: 4 servings.

*For steak sauce, we used A.1.

Broiling the ribs first browns them, adds **rich flavor,** and removes excess fat.

Grilled Ham and Apples

prep: 7 minutes   grill: 10 minutes

½   cup orange marmalade
2   teaspoons butter or margarine
¼   teaspoon ground ginger
2   (½-inch-thick) ham slices (about 2½ pounds)
4   small Granny Smith apples, cored and cut into
       4 rings each

Combine first 3 ingredients in a 1-cup glass measuring cup; microwave at HIGH 1 minute or until melted, stirring once.

Coat grill rack with cooking spray; place on grill over medium-high heat (350° to 400°). Place ham and apple rings on rack; grill, uncovered, 10 minutes or until apple rings are tender, turning and basting often with marmalade mixture. Yield: 6 to 8 servings.

Leave the peel on the apples for **pretty color.**

Creamy Ham Casserole

prep: 10 minutes   cook: 35 minutes

4   ounces dried medium egg noodles, uncooked
2   cups chopped cooked ham
1   medium-size green bell pepper, seeded and chopped
¼   cup chopped onion
¼   cup sliced celery
1   tablespoon vegetable oil
1   (10¾-ounce) can cream of mushroom soup, undiluted
1   (8-ounce) carton sour cream
½   cup (2 ounces) shredded Cheddar cheese

Cook pasta according to package directions; drain.
Cook ham and next 3 ingredients in oil in a large skillet over medium-high heat 5 minutes, stirring often.
Remove from heat; stir in soup, sour cream, and pasta.
Spoon into a lightly greased 1½-quart baking dish.
Cover and bake at 350° for 25 minutes. Sprinkle with cheese, and bake, uncovered, 5 more minutes. Let stand 10 minutes before serving. Yield: 4 servings.

Here's a great way to **use leftover ham.**

Toasted Almond Chicken

prep: 10 minutes   cook: 16 minutes

6 skinned and boned chicken breasts
1/8 teaspoon salt
1/8 teaspoon black pepper
3 tablespoons butter or margarine, divided
1 1/2 cups whipping cream
2 tablespoons orange marmalade
1 tablespoon Dijon mustard
1/8 teaspoon ground red pepper
1 (2.25-ounce) package sliced almonds, toasted

Place chicken between 2 sheets of heavy-duty plastic wrap, and flatten to 1/4-inch thickness, using a meat mallet or rolling pin. Sprinkle with salt and black pepper.

Melt 1 1/2 tablespoons butter in a large skillet over medium-high heat. Add half of chicken, and cook 2 minutes on each side or until golden. Remove chicken from skillet. Repeat procedure with remaining butter and chicken.

Reduce heat to medium; add whipping cream and next 3 ingredients to skillet, stirring well. Add chicken; sprinkle with almonds, and cook 8 minutes or until sauce thickens. Yield: 6 servings.

Toasting is an easy and quick way to bring out the **great flavor** in nuts.

Chicken Parmigiana

prep: 12 minutes   cook: 24 minutes

 4 skinned and boned chicken breasts
½ cup Italian-seasoned breadcrumbs
½ cup grated Parmesan cheese
 1 large egg, lightly beaten
 2 tablespoons butter or margarine
 1 (14-ounce) jar spaghetti sauce (about 2 cups)
 1 cup (4 ounces) shredded mozzarella cheese

Place chicken between 2 sheets of heavy-duty plastic wrap, and flatten to ¼-inch thickness, using a meat mallet or rolling pin.

Combine breadcrumbs and Parmesan cheese. Dip chicken in beaten egg; dredge in breadcrumb mixture.

Melt butter in a large skillet over medium-high heat; add chicken, and brown on each side. Arrange chicken in a lightly greased 11- x 7-inch baking dish. Pour spaghetti sauce over chicken, and sprinkle with mozzarella cheese. Cover and bake at 375° for 20 minutes or until thoroughly heated. Yield: 4 servings.

Use your favorite brand of spaghetti sauce in this recipe—**the spicier the better.**

Chicken-Almond Stir-Fry

prep: 6 minutes   cook: 10 minutes

2 tablespoons vegetable or sesame oil
4 skinned and boned chicken breasts, cut into thin strips
1 (2.25-ounce) package sliced almonds
1 (16-ounce) package frozen broccoli, carrots, and
    water chestnuts
1 tablespoon cornstarch
1 tablespoon brown sugar
½ teaspoon ground ginger
½ cup soy sauce
⅓ cup pineapple juice
Hot cooked rice

Pour oil around top of a preheated wok, coating sides, or in a large nonstick skillet. Heat briefly at medium-high (375°). Add chicken and almonds; stir-fry 2 minutes. Add frozen vegetables; cover and cook 4 minutes, stirring once.

Combine cornstarch and next 4 ingredients; add to wok. Cook, stirring constantly, 2 to 3 minutes or until mixture thickens. Serve over rice. Yield: 4 servings.

Here's a **one-dish meal** for sure—chicken, veggies, and rice.

Mama's Chicken Pot Pie

prep: 15 minutes   cook: 35 minutes

1   (10¾-ounce) can cream of celery or cream of
      chicken soup, undiluted
1½ cups chicken broth
3   cups chopped cooked chicken
1   (10-ounce) package frozen mixed vegetables
¼   teaspoon salt
¼   teaspoon pepper
½   cup butter
1   cup self-rising flour
¾   cup milk

Cook soup in a medium saucepan over medium heat until hot. Gradually add broth, stirring until smooth.
Add chicken, frozen vegetables, salt, and pepper. Bring to a boil; reduce heat, and simmer, uncovered, 10 minutes, stirring occasionally. Spoon mixture into a lightly greased 11- x 7-inch baking dish; set aside.
Cut butter into flour with a pastry blender or 2 knives until mixture is crumbly. Add ¾ cup milk, stirring just until dry ingredients are moistened. (Mixture will be lumpy.)
Gently spoon batter evenly on top of chicken mixture. Bake, uncovered, at 400° for 35 minutes or until golden.

This convenient pot pie uses frozen vegetables and an **easy homemade crust.**

Chicken Caesar Salad

prep: 10 minutes   cook: 6 minutes

¼ cup white wine vinegar
2 teaspoons Dijon mustard
1 teaspoon Worcestershire sauce
1½ pounds chicken breast strips (tenders)
1½ tablespoons lemon pepper
1 teaspoon garlic powder
¼ cup olive oil
8 cups tightly packed torn or shredded Romaine lettuce (about 1 medium head)
2 cups garlic croutons
½ cup shredded Parmesan cheese

Combine first 3 ingredients, stirring well; set aside. **Dredge** chicken in lemon pepper and garlic powder. Pour oil into a large skillet, and place over medium-high heat until hot. Cook chicken in hot oil 5 minutes or until done, turning once. Remove chicken from skillet, reserving drippings in skillet; drain chicken on paper towels. Remove skillet from heat; stir vinegar mixture into reserved drippings, scraping particles that cling to bottom of skillet. Pour warm vinegar dressing over lettuce; add chicken, and toss. Sprinkle with croutons and cheese. Yield: 4 servings.

Most stores sell **strips of chicken breast** labeled as tenders, but if not, cut your own from boneless breasts.

Nacho Chicken

prep: 5 minutes   cook: 25 minutes

    2   tablespoons mayonnaise
    ¼   teaspoon salt
    ¼   teaspoon dried Italian seasoning
    2   skinned and boned chicken breasts
    ¾   cup crushed nacho cheese-flavored tortilla chips
        (about 30)
    1   tablespoon butter or margarine, melted

Combine first 3 ingredients; spread on both sides of chicken. Dredge chicken in crushed chips. Place chicken on a lightly greased baking sheet or jellyroll pan, and drizzle with butter. Bake at 350° for 20 to 25 minutes or until chicken is done. Yield: 2 servings.

Kids love this crispy chicken breaded with nacho-flavored chips.

Turkey Pie

prep: 12 minutes   cook: 45 minutes

½ (15-ounce) package refrigerated piecrusts
3 large eggs, lightly beaten
1 cup (4 ounces) shredded sharp Cheddar cheese,
   divided
2 cups chopped cooked turkey
⅓ cup chopped onion
⅓ cup chicken broth
¼ cup half-and-half
¼ cup mayonnaise
2 tablespoons all-purpose flour
¼ teaspoon salt
¼ teaspoon pepper
3 drops of hot sauce
1 (8-ounce) container sour cream

Fit piecrust into a 9-inch pieplate according to package directions; fold edges under, and crimp. Prick bottom and sides lightly with a fork. Bake at 400° for 10 minutes.

Combine eggs, ½ cup cheese, turkey, and remaining 9 ingredients in a large bowl, stirring until blended; pour into prepared crust. Bake, uncovered, at 400° for 20 minutes. Reduce oven temperature to 350°. Bake 10 to 15 more minutes or until set; sprinkle with remaining ½ cup cheese for last 2 minutes of baking. Yield: 6 servings.

Leftover turkey is a prize in this easy, cheesy meat pie.

Zesty Fish Po'boys

prep: 20 minutes

2 (11-ounce) packages frozen breaded fish fillets
2 (12-inch) French bread loaves
1 cup regular or light mayonnaise
3 tablespoons lemon juice
1 tablespoon Creole mustard
1 tablespoon sweet pickle relish
1 teaspoon chopped fresh or ½ teaspoon dried
 parsley
¼ teaspoon dried tarragon
½ teaspoon hot sauce
4 lettuce leaves

Bake fish fillets according to package directions. Set aside, and keep warm.

Cut bread in half crosswise. Split each half lengthwise, and toast.

Stir together mayonnaise and next 6 ingredients. Spread mixture evenly over cut sides of bread halves. Place lettuce and fish on bottom bread halves; top with remaining bread halves. Serve immediately. Yield: 4 servings.

Note: For testing purposes only, we used Gorton's Southern Fried Country Style Breaded Fish Fillets.

So easy. So quick. **So yummy.**

Delta-Style Fried Catfish

prep: 20 minutes   chill: 8 hours
stand: 10 minutes   cook: 4 minutes per batch

1½ cups milk
 2 to 3 drops hot sauce
 6 (4- to 6-ounce) catfish fillets
 ¾ cup yellow cornmeal
 ¼ cup all-purpose flour
 2 teaspoons salt
 1 teaspoon ground black pepper
 1 teaspoon ground red pepper
 ¼ teaspoon garlic powder
Vegetable oil

Whisk together milk and hot sauce. Place catfish fillets in a single layer in a 13- x 9-inch baking dish, and cover with milk mixture. Cover and chill 8 hours, turning once.

Combine cornmeal and next 5 ingredients in a shallow dish, and set aside.

Let catfish fillets stand at room temperature in milk mixture in baking dish 10 minutes. Remove fillets from milk mixture, allowing excess to drip off.

Dredge fillets in cornmeal mixture, shaking off excess.

Pour oil to a depth of 1½ inches into a large, deep cast-iron or heavy-duty skillet; heat to 360°. Fry fillets, in batches, 2 minutes on each side or until golden brown. Remove to a wire rack on a paper towel-lined jellyroll pan. Keep warm in a 225° oven until ready to serve. Yield: 6 servings.

This true Southern dish gets **a little kick** from hot sauce and ground red pepper.

Shrimp Creole

prep: 8 minutes   cook: 10 minutes

    2 tablespoons butter or margarine
    ½ cup chopped green bell pepper
    ¼ cup chopped celery
    4 green onions, thinly sliced
    1 garlic clove, minced
    1 (14½-ounce) can Cajun-style stewed tomatoes,
       undrained
    1 (6-ounce) can tomato paste
    ½ cup water
    2 teaspoons dried parsley flakes
    ½ teaspoon chicken bouillon granules
    ½ teaspoon salt
    ¼ teaspoon ground red pepper
    1 pound peeled, medium-size fresh shrimp (1⅓ pounds
       unpeeled)
    Hot cooked rice

Melt butter in a large skillet over medium-high heat; add green pepper and next 3 ingredients. Cook, stirring constantly, 4 minutes. Add tomatoes and next 6 ingredients; cook 2 minutes over medium heat. Add shrimp, and cook 4 minutes or until shrimp turn pink. Serve over rice. Yield: 3 to 4 servings.

Cajun-style tomatoes provide much of the seasoning in this simple favorite.

Artichoke and Shrimp Linguine

prep: 4 minutes   cook: 18 minutes

    8 ounces dried linguine, uncooked
    ¼ cup olive oil
    1 pound peeled, medium-size fresh shrimp (1 ⅓ pounds
       unpeeled)
    ½ teaspoon dried crushed red pepper
    3 garlic cloves, minced
    1 (14-ounce) can quartered artichoke hearts, drained
    1 (2¼-ounce) can sliced ripe olives, drained
    ¼ cup lemon juice
    ⅛ teaspoon salt
    ⅛ teaspoon pepper
    ½ cup grated Parmesan cheese

Cook pasta according to package directions; drain and
keep warm in a large bowl.
Meanwhile, heat oil in a large skillet over medium-
high heat until hot; add shrimp, red pepper, and garlic. Cook, stirring constantly, 3 to 5 minutes or until
shrimp turn pink. Stir in artichoke hearts and next 4
ingredients; cook just until thoroughly heated. Add
artichoke mixture to pasta, and sprinkle with cheese.
Yield: 4 servings.

Sauté the shrimp mixture while the pasta cooks,
and **dinner's ready in half the time.**

Seafood Cakes

prep: 30 minutes   cook: 16 minutes   chill: 1 hour

½ pound unpeeled, medium-size fresh shrimp
½ pound grouper or other lean white fish fillets
½ cup diced onion
¼ cup diced celery
¼ cup diced green bell pepper
1 tablespoon mayonnaise
1 tablespoon butter or margarine, melted
1 large egg
1 teaspoon Old Bay seasoning
2 teaspoons Worcestershire sauce
½ teaspoon paprika
¼ teaspoon salt
¼ teaspoon dried crushed red pepper
¼ teaspoon ground black pepper
½ pound fresh crabmeat, drained and flaked*
3 cups soft breadcrumbs, divided
2 tablespoons butter or margarine
2 tablespoons vegetable oil
1¼ cups tartar sauce

Peel shrimp; devein, if desired.

Arrange shrimp and grouper in a steamer basket over boiling water. Cover and steam 10 minutes or until grouper flakes easily with a fork. Cool and chop shrimp and grouper.

Combine onion and next 11 ingredients; stir in shrimp mixture, crabmeat, and 1 cup breadcrumbs.

Shape mixture into 12 patties; coat with remaining 2 cups breadcrumbs. Cover and chill 1 hour.

Melt 2 tablespoons butter in oil in a large skillet over medium heat; add patties, and cook 3 minutes on each side or until golden. Drain on paper towels, and serve with tartar sauce. Yield: 6 servings.

*Substitute 1 (6-ounce) can lump crabmeat, drained, for fresh crabmeat, if desired.

Spice up store-bought tartar sauce by stirring in a diced jalapeño pepper.

Black Beans and Yellow Rice

prep: 4 minutes   cook: 23 minutes

1   (5-ounce) package saffron rice mix
1   (15-ounce) can black beans
3   tablespoons lime juice
1   teaspoon chili powder
½   teaspoon ground cumin
2   tablespoons chopped fresh cilantro, divided
Garnishes: sour cream, sliced green onions

Cook rice according to package directions; keep warm. Meanwhile, drain beans, reserving 2 table-spoons liquid. Combine beans, reserved liquid, lime juice, chili powder, and cumin in a saucepan. Cook over medium heat until thoroughly heated; stir in 1 tablespoon cilantro.

Serve beans over rice, and sprinkle with remaining 1 tablespoon cilantro. Garnish, if desired. Yield: 3 servings.

Rice mix, a can of beans, and a few simple sea-sonings become **a vegetarian delight.**

Tortilla Pie

prep: 11 minutes   cook: 25 minutes

 1 (16-ounce) can refried beans or black beans, drained
 1 teaspoon chili powder
½ teaspoon ground cumin
 8 (8-inch) flour tortillas
 1 cup chunky salsa
 2 (4- or 6-ounce) cartons guacamole
 1 (8-ounce) package shredded Mexican cheese blend
Garnishes: sour cream, additional salsa and guacamole

Combine first 3 ingredients, stirring well.

Place 1 tortilla in a lightly greased 9-inch round cakepan; spread with half of bean mixture, and top with another tortilla. Spread with ½ cup salsa, and top with another tortilla. Spread with half of guacamole, and top with another tortilla. Sprinkle with half of cheese, and top with another tortilla.

Repeat layers with remaining ingredients, except cheese. (Pan will be full.) Cover and bake at 350° for 20 minutes; uncover and sprinkle with remaining cheese.

Bake, uncovered, 3 to 5 more minutes. Cut into wedges to serve. Garnish, if desired. Yield: 6 servings.

Your salsa selection can **spice things up** or tone things down in this recipe.

index